PATIENT FRAME

PATIENT FRAME

STEVEN HEIGHTON

POEMS

ANANSI

This edition published in 2010 by
House of Anansi Press Inc.
110 Spadina Avenue, Suite 801
Toronto, ON, M5V 2K4
Tel. 416-363-4343
Fax 416-363-1017
www.anansi.ca

Distributed in Canada by
HarperCollins Canada Ltd.
1995 Markham Road
Scarborough, ON, M1B 5M8
Toll free tel. 1-800-387-0117

Distributed in the United States by
Publishers Group West
1700 Fourth Street
Berkeley, CA 94710
Toll free tel. 1-800-788-3123

House of Anansi Press is committed to protecting our natural environment.
As part of our efforts, this book is printed on paper that contains 100%
post-consumer recycled fibres, is acid-free, and is processed chlorine-free.

14 13 12 11 10   1 2 3 4 5

LIBRARY AND ARCHIVES CANADA CATALOGUING IN PUBLICATION

Heighton, Steven
Patient frame / Steven Heighton.

Poems.
ISBN 978-0-88784-952-7

I. Title.

PS8565.E451P37 2010   C811'.54   C2009-906398-0

Library of Congress Control Number: 2009939250

Cover design: Bill Douglas at The Bang
Text design and typesetting: Ingrid Paulson

 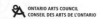

*We acknowledge for their financial support of our publishing program
the Canada Council for the Arts, the Ontario Arts Council,
and the Government of Canada through the Canada Book Fund.*

Printed and bound in Canada

CONTENTS

It is very strange that the years teach us patience—-
that the shorter our time, the greater our capacity for waiting.

—Elizabeth Taylor, *A Wreath of Roses*

Monstrous acts are fundamentally impatient.

—Stamatis Smyrlis

1

CREDOS

ANOTHER OF THE JUST: WARRANT OFFICER HUGH THOMPSON, MY LAI, 1968

Years later, sober, or from inside the snub barrel
of a shot glass, you spoke out about it softly,
not reticent but baffled, still: how Calley

and his men appeared below you, butchering
the villagers, and down you banked your recon
chopper to light between him and the enemy

women, toddlers, crones. Ordered your door-gunners
to fire on any comrades who'd resume that riot
of infanticide, mob rape—and then, from a midden

of twitching limbs, your crew pried free a gore-smeared child
and bore him beyond harm, as if *to save* was also labour
for male arms, as if love were the one flag you'd salute.

(Not quite—you were a keen recruit, proudly hailed patriot.)
You're gone now, cancer, my sad captain, while Calley—
a few years' house arrest for four hundred dead—lives

in Atlanta, retired. *Don't do something in hope of reward,*
you said, *it might never come.* Just lynch mail, roadkill,
razored strays splayed at your door. Still, in the Agent

Orange skies, your archangelic contrail lingers—you
at the flightstick, bearing the one child. Forget the pen,
forget the sword: the strongest hands hold neither, but they hold.

BREATHE LIKE THIS

He was in a terrible state—that of consciousness.
Some while ago in his life he had lost the knack
of choosing what to think about.
                    —Martin Amis, *The Information*

Each day an hour in heaven, an hour in hell.
First: peopled scenes, how even our quarrels
or stalemate silences are coupling of a kind
and parole from the hellself: cellblock walls
are balsa compared. Pry me open. The skull
a chatroom run by monkeys, chittering, stoned,
a roach hotel, round-the-clock arcade, a gym
for obsessives, shadow boxing. And in the end:
that haiku helm where fields' last cricket grieves
summer in a voice faint as a codicil.

Then comes that other hour, when my love revives—
when rain falls like a ransom through the hymn-
soft stillness of a mind waking to wonders small
as the ounce of breath Alison Krauss sighs in
before she sings *As I went down to the river*
to pray, or prayer itself, or the horizon
of desire your bedded body makes in cool
silhouette, deep nights, dispelling hell. Sever
nothing from here on—couple this to that. Unselved
is unsplit,
                    and to breathe like this is to be absolved.

JETLAG

June, Arkhangel'sk

It's night in your bones   though noon. A no one
room, drugged with sunlight of a skewed
latitude,
the fizz in capillaries behind the eyes' red rind, un-

housed, stalling hydraulics of the heart. The insomniac
lens of the sun deepens this lag, and   dizzies, is dis-
inclined to set, reset this
body clock,

wonky, jarred as a man who bends to rinse
his face clean of a night's journey and straightens
to meet himself above the sink: no mirror, his face
drywall. Such times a phantom tourist

might urge to mind moments that lodge you
deep in a life:
                when you first heard last century's best tenor,
Jussi Björling, skewer the skynote in "O Helga Natt," and swore
no more lies and of course still lied but less and less as years
went and years went and that high C went on
compounding in your soul, or
                for the first time kissed her breasts in the fire-alley
of a mountain town, under the startled brainwaves

of the aurora borealis
                or hiked the low cliffs of Naxos with the child
on your back, her weight bracing your step to soil
so at last you felt present—sheathed in sheer being—
she chanting the genesis of all she spied,
lending back through the ear's narrowed estuary
that urgent inventory—

these things you summon to seeing, to rudder you
in the real   in a no one room
with night in your bones——

RIBS

With their passion for western rock teased, music lovers tried desperately to get
their hands on recorded material. Because there were very few pressing plants —
and because state music releases were so tightly controlled — an industrious fow
converted old record players into record-cutters, using discarded hospital X-Rays for
plastic (the emulsion on the X-Rays' surface was perfect for sound reproduction).
For decades, much of the Soviet populace first heard Western rock bands on "ribs" —
prototypical, 7-inch flexi-discs (Roentgenizdat) played at 78 rpm and purchased
for kopecks (pennies) at most hospitals.

          —Dave Bidini, *Around the World in 57 ½ Gigs*

Record these fragments, now
seeming mere figments, fused
briefly back to sound—
                      the urgent queue at Emerg, clamouring
not for medical help
but music,
          clumsy drunk in traction
whose wrecked skeleton at 78 dances
        to the Dead, jitters to The Turtles
and The Doors,
                the cabbie with the skull fracture
that Kinks and Ventures rollick out of
        as if from the stubborn radio
of his shattered Lada,
                in a raingrey ward
the circus starlet, all sensation
          neuter below the hips, who sockhops
a few hundred turns on Santa Barbara sands

to the Beach Boys,
              the boy   whose pulverized fingers
        in phantom negative   pick with Hendrix
          a psychotropic, screeching feedback riff,
                all pain reprieved
                all song as opiate, solace that forms
      and soars from the grooves and nerves
        of this forked, frail sack of bones, briefly
            marrowed with music—

                          Babushka whose honeycombed hips
      shimmy a last time to the Stones,
                the star prospect for Spartak or Dynamo
            whose femoral break—a scratch in the vinyl
                blurred on the turntable—seems now
              spliced back to solid
                          and plays on

THE NEITHER LIFE

Those who are not
   too cold or too hot
travel straight into Hamelin
            —Marina Tsvetaeva, *The Ratcatcher*

Hypocrite commuter
You have a house on both shores
         a home on neither
Two families
         no loved ones
A pact with the somnambulist
         gods of the vine
         and keys to the early bird city of Hamelin —

City without qualm without quandary
         not too cold not too hot,
         neither vesicle nor icicle,
         fascicle nor flame,
         not bloodshed or Buddha,
                              Hell,
here, is this neither life, zero sum
         accommodation, where the wasps
         are weaving hives
         into the dead eyes
         of the streetlamps —

OUTRAM LAKE

Lake buried under the Hope Slide, Hope, B.C., January 1965

The rhyme of your death revives the couplet.

No one's with you on the porch the bitter night
   you submit yourself to winter, to wed,
      with ice, your absence
to a buried wife's, dying toward her
   in a way that's anaesthetic
      and yet, in its simple dignity, aesthetic too—
that would matter to you—
   while in the vital, summerlike hum
      of sodium streetlamps, a cold confetti of snowflakes
settles homeward, marking this reunion, till it's time
   and timeless, the lush numbness of freezing
      stills you, and your lips and fingers
are done versing.
                    A cold spring
and we drive from the coast into the Cascades
to witness how a body of water can vanish:
                                   this prior loss
could hardly have rhymed less—deafening,
fast—massed panzers of boulders and snow
loosing downvalley over a doomed throughway
to plough traffic under, then bombarding

onward to bury Outram Lake, ages
deep, under a jumbled slag
like dense, enigmatic wording.

(*wait for me   in that winter room*—)

Different, yet here too a beauty
interred, flow stalled (we thought at first),
until, miles downvalley, reading in the car,
we came to ourselves along a glacial stream
braiding green with subconscious silts
from under time's not quite decisive slide—

Richard Outram, poet, died Port Hope, 21 January 2005

What good the words
if not to try, to sing
a route through
to that August room, summon
the origins, pane of hail,
kiss of smoke, invoke
the chance, uncallable
gods who got them there
and let them stay,
still famished, a day
a night a further day,
meshed glances stunned
as a couple drowning
in capricorn surf
of sheets kicked askew . . .
                              Out past
where diction fathoms depth,
still swimming, limbs
still oaring, they're mute now
but not in sleep, sleep's
unreachable in such fraught
vicinities, when they try,
the barest nudge or stroke
jilts both awake to this same
aching sacrament—
                         And reach,

by dawn of the second day, a point
where glances, even, are injury,
the world's annulled,
absolved beyond two
bodies who clutch and come
to the archipelago's last
pulse of land, their heartbeats, too,
in tidal lock now,
slowing.
      So yield
to humid lagoons of sleep
and silence, till it be crucial
to speak of this again, or
sing, and what good the words
if not to sing——

SOME OTHER JUST ONES

a footnote to Borges

The printer who sets this page with skill, though he may not admire it.
Singers of solo expertise who defer and find harmonies instead.
Anyone whose skeleton is susceptible to music.
She who, having loved a book or record, instantly passes it on.
Whose heart lilts at a span of vacant highway, the fervent surge
    of acceleration, psalm of the tires.
Adults content to let children bury them in sand or leaves.
Those for whom sustaining hatred is a difficulty.
Surprised by tenderness on meeting, at a reunion, the persecutors
    of their youth.
Likely to forget debts owed them but never a debt they owe.
Apt to read Plutarch or Thich Naht Hahn with the urgency of one
    reading the morning news.
Frightened ones who fight to keep fear from keeping them from life.
The barber who, no matter how long the line, will not rush the
    masterful shave or cut.
The small-scale makers of precious obscurios—pomegranate spoons,
    conductors' batons, harpsichord tuning hammers, War of 1812
    re-enactors' ramrods, hand-cranks for hurdy-gurdies.
The gradeschool that renewed the brownfields back of the A & P
    and made them ample miraculous May and June.
The streetgang that casts no comment as they thin out to let Bob
    the barking man squawk past them on the sidewalk.
The two African medical students in Belgrade, 1983, who seeing a
    traveller lost and broke took him in and fed him rice and
    beans cooked over a camp stove in their cubicle of a room
    and let him sleep there while one of them studied all night
    at the desk between the beds with the lamp swung low.

Those who sit on front porches, not in fenced privacy, in the
    erotic inaugural summer night steam.
Who redeem from neglect a gorgeous, long-orphaned word.
Who treat dogs with a sincere and comical diplomacy.
Attempt to craft a decent wine in a desperate climate.
Clip the chain of consequence by letting others have the last word.
Master the banjo.
Are operatically loud in love.
These people, without knowing it, are saving the world.

2

SELECTED MONSTERS

SELECTED MONSTERS

for Barbara Gowdy

In Florence, circa 1460, Cosimo de' Medici enclosed a mixed group of animals in a
pen and invited Pope Pius II to attend the spectacle, which was meant to determine
which beast was the most ferocious: the lion, the fighting bull, the bloodhound, the
gorilla, or perhaps the giraffe—an animal then known in Europe as a Camelopard.

"Holiness, with these monsters in close quarters
we're sure to have a brawl." But the new Caesars
lacked some Roman secret—razors

in the stable straw, or a bonus
bout of starvation, glass goads in the anus
or a goon squad of trainers

who knew how to crack a good whip.
So this static, comic crèche—this flop—
a Peaceable Kingdom with cud-chewing bull, ape

absently wanking, lion asleep, bloodhound's
limbs twitching in some wet dream of a hind's
stotting fetlocks, and the giraffe, free of wounds,

hunched by the fence, its trembling yellow ass
not enough to coax an assault. Pius
cleared his throat. "The Florence heat, I suppose,"

he yawned. "I've seen sportier feats
at a Synod. When's dinner?" Trailing hoots
and loutcalls, the mob drained out at the exits,

the boxseats emptied, the media crews
taxied elsewhere, till finally Cosimo's
bloodpit was a high-shelved archive of human refuse—

handbills, tickets, peanut shells, all set to motion
by a new wind, as if performing for that pen
of blinking inmates, who remained there . . . still remain

in the blinding empirical lens of the sun
and uranium rainfall, centuries on.
                                        "At eight.
Expect exotic cuts. And excellent wine."

COLLISION

Away in the eyefar
nightrise over the sapwood, and one likes
under hooves the heatfeel after run flees, heat stays on this
smooth to the hoof hardpan, part trail
part saltlick now as snowlast moults back
into the sapwood
to yard and rot
and one sees moonrise mounding
over a groundswell, but too soon and swifter
like never the moon one knows, no moon at all,
two moons fawned, both small, too hot, they
come with a growling and
hold one fast, so chafing for flight
but what, what, what, what
wondering——

and one can't move and can't although one
knows from backdays, eared and glimpsed
through sapwood budwood cracklewood bonewood
flashes of this same Wolfing
                                        now upon one, still
stalls the hooves on the saltlick and the eyebright
creature squeals   afraid?——and one somehow
uphoofed in a bound not chosen high as if to flee with no
trying, no feeling, fallen   flankflat, fawnlike

eyes above in the eyefar closing small
with the world

                        and now from the stopped thing
comes what   its cub?   legged up on its hinds,
kneels low to touch, but in that awful
touch, no feel   no fear to feel
no at all——

NIGHTMARE

I will be standing
on the verge of a plain
by a highway

Flat dance of the skyline
skin seared by a treeless sun
somewhere the roar of ocean

                          or a silver car
that slows   stops
a door that swings

and I must choose
on the verge of the plain—
and though it is hard to see

through the layering dust
I believe I hoist my bag and
pull it after me

into that car

"THAR HE"

Roy Bryant's deathbed confession

We was acquitted and then, protected
by the laws, we sold our story—how for hours
we beat that boy witless and then shot and
weighed him down in the river. Told jokes on it
too, at the time. "Aint it just like a nigger
to try swimming the Tallahatchee with half
a cotton gin on his back?" Four thousand, they paid—
most I seen in my lifetime, before or since.
Some reckon thats when the Lord stepped in. I dont.
Not when all we done is our natural
duty as husbands, and the Lord God, He must
of knowed it.
                          But something changed then. The others
closed down my store by shunning it. Across
all the South come changes, folks so vexed up
by a single death—and his Daddy a rapist,
you ever know that? Why dont them city
liberals ever say? Changes come, and me and
J. W. reap up the blame. I leave the state,
lose my store, my house, kids, my high school queen,
lose my sight, too, in time, like maybe other
women aint worth the seeing now. Anyhow
its best, I reckon, not to see Death coming . . .
or to see you all here now, inquiring
about whats so long dead and done. That boy just

never ought to wet his lips to whistle. And
you all, ganged round me with questions—what is this
wrong digging, this killing hunger? Hell with you.
You all tell me that boy was young? In the hours
till he died, he grew younger and younger.

While my friend (the kid
you misconducted—the boy you left
songless in a sexton's yard among the open
doors of dug graves, among which he passed
the rest of a life curtailed, half-
cursed) coughed
and edged toward his solo
consummation, sir, you did zero
but soil other choirboys in your charge, and coyly
charm, flirt with the mothers, eventually
passing some pensive months in minimum—
society claiming its pound of flesh, to quote
just one of your hack apologists (the boy
himself is now an ounce of dust)—
where, I ungraciously suppose, you must
have checked your mirrored face, to rehearse the miens
of remorse, that sanctimonious sideshow,
along with other states of which your choir used to descant
in the superb manner you, a fine teacher, taught well: *repent*,
for example, or *atone*,
which to you must have sounded too much like *alone*
(a place where you're saddled with your own soul
and nobody there to perform for, fool
or abuse). Hard time! Tonight, sir, I still accuse
you, who—while earth slowly unstrings a boy
in his *lento* measure of staved ground—
still savours the tang

of August tomatoes, chords of Fauré's *Requiem*
(two years served, in fairway minimum)
and the rectifying esteem of upstanding Ang-
lican pals. So in your pool or Jacuzzi
wallow pink as a gangster, as water
bubbles like laughter, or the last
cantique of boy sopranos
vanished into their lives—bass now, tenor—
or through some colder
one way door.

For days afterward, all talk and blog
was of the shootout, but about your condition
not even Google gave a clue.
Were you still in ICU, were you now in the morgue
(your ancient cadaver under guard) or recovering—
good to stand and spritz a jury with soapbox spittle?
One thing was sure and that was zero contrition.
Some say you killed and then fell quoting a little
Ezra Pound—braying in tall font about the elders of Zion
(with their Aryan stooges) running the banks and the Fed.
Some said this, some said that, but none knew if you were dying
or on the mend, or even, once again, spry.
Race traitors want to see me dead
but I'm not the kind to die.

        Hang on a minute, wait, I always heard hate
was supposed to kill a guy,
honeycomb the bones, lace the blood, leave the heart
a cold pinch of tailings, while love—well,
love was like live-forever ginseng, a T-cell
tonic. You make me rethink so many thoughts.
Shot in face, exit wound all but severing spine,
and for your 89th birthday they take you off saline
and O_2, like a nursed preemie nearly good to go—
a clean start—at least in one report. But hell,
someone around here ought to know.
Is the oldest man in the world still alive?
Race traitors try to take me down
but I'm not the kind to die.

EACH MAN KILLS THE THING HE LOVES

He relives the collision through the eyes
of the deer, drunk, days later, *The deer*
knows my eyes for what they are —
halogen beams groping uproad, blinkered
along the broken or solid, through bracken
mist in the dips, always hurried — glued
to the future — not seeing the way
for the highway.
      She knows me the way prey
knows predator, peers through gritted grilles
into engines of blind appetite, while killer, losing prey
in the killing, knows less, like a quantum seeker
stalking particles
his instruments can't pin.

All the same, he thinks, it's only a.
Thinks, forget the deductible, I could have been.
Thinks, another beer, a shot, something won't quite.

(Kneels and the downed doe's eye
contains his stooped face like a locket, opened
look, look, the beloved — before it seals.)

"No good to make a mask of forgiving.
I still hate your guts, hate your DNA. You're
coreless, conceited, glutted with callous fun.
You never praised anyone
until others did first. You're your own miscreation,
you're an animate stain.
(Mosquitoes, like vampires, hide from the sun.)
Whoever's stock is stalling you prance in with your kicks,
icepick-heeled, high-chinned in vain
pride of your paltry sinecure, your salon
of pale fawners. Lady, I hate you.
You tried to steal my living.
When you titter, you swell and quiver like aspic.
When you laugh, I hear dregs glugging down a loud drain."

CONSTANCE & HER STALKERS

In the end, sometimes, starvation simply arrests the heart.
　　　—Jean Takamura, *Hungers*

Useless, useless,
　sign the hands of the assassin
　　hunted down in the straw.

Or the searchteam's
　pilot in the typhoon
　　forgetting his horizon.

Useless the locks on
　windows, doors.
　　Helpless the law.

Constance was always on the cusp
of something crazy, her windows, doors
unlocked while a casual
strangler cased the trailer parks
and dirt lanes fringing Reno.

　　We warned her, but she was starving
　　and it sapped her concentration.

Wish you lived in the world sometimes,
I told her, foraging in the minus hours
through her phantom pantry,
empty. James Brown steaming in stereo;
neat Tanqueray. She said,
We can do dark
another day, nothing ever
has to be relived.

Under adobe
listening to the desert
wind's weird tunings, remote
wasping of a pilot, miles higher,
surveillant—maybe an eye
on the man in the news,
that failed assassin and
feared (by the sane)
assailant.

> She said she was surviving
> but there was talk of an operation.

To what were you constant?
Your hunger. Lurid maroon
tattoo of forearm scars,
that wreck in progress.

Sincere nihilist.

I saw myself complacent, un-
grateful for all earth had given.

When I came, I came like judgement.

That night, the strangler again
struck the outskirts, again
failing, just, to kill, but laying down
further strata of fear.
The reason why I'm here.
Near dawn I ran home
down a scorpion turnpike
and a squadcar slowed and coasted
beside me, the face in there
probing, the beacon's
coronary strobing
lighting a broken
arc of the desert floor——

THE MASCOT

The installation / a comic strip head on its side on a white plinth /
deflated, small pink body clumped on the floor like a sloughed or flayed
skin / in the corner a dark Flintstone cudgel propped against the wall /

I am alone in this cartoon,
                                 take my history: fable
of every-mascot, everyman, woman, adrift
in the thin atmosphere high on this plinth,
like that desert saint roosting years on a pillar
in old Syria—vulture of his own slow mortification—
and what do we have against the body, anyway?

My story: cartoon head on a pedestal, though no longer
limestone, marble, Socrates or Sappho,
that archaic torso of Apollo,
                                 far between the comfy
caravanserais of galaxies, how I miss the home planet,
my body. It lies remote below, sloughed and shucked
like a superhero suit, though pink, not blue,
with smog and assorted   nautical toxins.

Start the telling in cavelit millennia, eras of flint of cudgel of
coughing soot and no escape from the palpably
dying flesh, the trembling in pelts, nursing burns, wolfing

other flesh raw—but also starting to outline in ochre and ashes
those first surging, sacred beasts, there beside the living
shadows of hands—starting to petal the husks of the dead
in their permafrost graves with gentian, rue
and bluebells.
          Our dead.
                      Ice-sheets long as the Tigris withdrew, blue,
cold-blooded behemoths leery of our growing fires,
light, language, etchings—as if these miracles decreed their retreat!
In the thawing vales, first furrows appeared, harvests. First towns.
First cities. First comforts. Apparently life was to be more
than a brute bout with hypothermia and big
diligent predators.
                In our cavewall cartoons
our heads had been mere nubs—puny afterthoughts—our physiques
thick and large, wishfully well-fed. Now heads were growing
to proportion. Already: cuneiform scribes, accountants, astronomers, spies,
touts, troubadours, personal trainers, tort lawyers, stand-up comics in
          jingling hats,
sculptors who would gouge (we're in Greece now) marble busts
with eyes blank as Modigliani's—because the *whole*
person was what saw, with body/mind still welded,
saw and thought and conceived——
                   All those generations
our sensed enterprise was somehow to drag our being
into balance, muscled hunter and pensive angel, amorous phantom.
Eliot thought we'd arrived once, in Donne, Shakespeare, Marlowe,
         those few
thinking their feelings and feeling their thought—

not quite, no, not nearly, though we were getting somewhere.
But the head grew onward, with the tumorous ego (sealed
habitat of hubris),
                          and we had ways now,
a little learning, exponential technologies—
we had Nature, at last, pinned down.
And the head kept swelling, packing
a madness of data / metastatic taxonomies /
the hoarder's drive to confiscate, control. . . .

Here I tilt, perfected emblem, effigy of the age,
on my column surfing my own brainwaves
like one adrift in a video game. Hair cyan-blue, huge
spongiform eyes, head sidewise staring upward
in some consternation, apparently, alone in this cartoon
and missing earth, my flesh, the sourcewater
brooks of the blood,
                          I should have
danced more and drawn fewer blueprints.

Chief Inquisitor
Torquemada, 83, died
In his sleep, deep
In a featherbed
Dream, fellated
With praise
By church, state and
Street, enveloped
In honours and (you
Have to think)
Indian silks—maybe
There is no Karma?
—Still
I call on whatever
Light and good
There is, to quit
Dozing over Oprah
After rosé lunches,
Texting, riffling
Forms at the desk
Of the celestial
Bureaucracy
And receive this humble
Urgent request

To act, or rather
Don't—do not
Take this one away
From her—you see
I ask not that things
Be given to the friend
I love, but rather:
Let her expectant
Dream remain (unlike
The last few) un-
Reclaimed by earth,
Unrecalled to heaven,
Or wherever,
Please.

Herewith I
Submit my simple
Prayer for Heather.

3

ELEGIES & OTHER LOVE SONGS

HOME MOVIES, 8 mm

What holds you here, besides small shocks
of delight, then embarrassment, seeing these too-fast
films unravelling, mute but for the sprockets'
plastic chatter, an outboard roar as the almost-

antique projector, Yashica 1965, splashes clips
of faces in their once-loved form (forgotten
till now — interred in the nerves) on screen. What keeps
you here tensed, if not frustration

at your impotence to intervene — reach back
and brace the hand holding the camera that pans
away, again, with a young hand's
impatience to contain all: slaphammer first home, a block

of Main Street rising between houses
to a mine's brontosaur headframe, in the laser-
blue noon of subarctic winter —
then, in a dress-coat the colour of roses,

a mother, breaking the frame, waving a newsreel's
sped-up wave, while from the left a dog lollops in,
unrecalled as ever so small,
so awkward! — and you rush the screen,

kneel closer and again the camera
swivels away—
stout neighbour in dark overcoat and fedora,
mouth going—while to the left you can almost *see*

her and that dog in the dark, or wherever the place
is, forty years out of frame (both dead now), as the man in the coat
tips his hat and the scene cuts, to white. Greece
then, Nipissing, faces in flashes, the light

sallowed, even children stained by that ambery
tone, as the lens pivots faster, refuses focus,
close-up, the patient frame. I know memory,
what these reels were meant to fortress,

aims the same fickle lens, leaving gaps and blurs
in the record, but what of the eye itself, as it glides
over a lifetime's loves the same way—careless
and rushed, a manic amateur—

and the little reel clicks down inside?

If I could start over, I would stare and stare.

The woman whose eyesight is fading tries to read
her son's first book. It's long, 300 pages,
of which she can take in a page a night, at best.
When the doctor says she has less than a year

it's not her eyesight he means. As she reads, death
gets on with its own determined work—studying,
mastering the subtle codes, transcribing her
cell by syllable into the dense, vast anthology

of the dead. Death never doubts itself, as her son,
she knows, must do. Death gets it right each time.
She reads till all sense stops rising from the page,

this plot no lamp can brighten. A week's worth left
to be unveiled. In the still-encrypted world
she and her son the last reader and writer.

There's a final bedtime when the father reads
to his daughter under the half-moon lamp.
The wolf-eyed dog sits guard on the snowy
quilt at their feet—ears pricked, head upright
like a dragon on its hoard—while the daughter's
new clock ticks on the dresser. When the father
shuts the book, neither feels in the cool sigh
cast from its pages a breath of the end—
and how can it be that this ritual
will not recur? True, this latest story
is over, *Treasure Island*, which held them
a dozen nights, but "the end" has arrived
this way often before. Maybe she's tired
of the rite, or waking to a sense of herself
revised? Maybe he's temporarily bored,
or unmoored, reading by duty or rote,
turning deeper inside his own concerns.

How does the end enter? There's a hinging
like a book's sewn spine in the raw matter
of time—that coded text, illegible—
and stretched too far, it goes. An innocent
break, the father gone one weekend or the child
sleeping at a friend's, followed by a night

or two she wants to read alone, or write,
for a change, in her new padlock journal.
She has no idea what has changed. She
can't know that the enlargement of her life
demands small death after death, and this one,
the latest, is far from last. She will not
notice this death, being so intent on life—
so implied in its stretching crewelwork
of seconds.
              Some nights later, suddenly,
writing cheques or checking email, he might
notice and wonder at the change. In a sense
such minor passings pre-enact his own.
For a moment he might lay down his pen,
forget the figures, peer over the roofline
and find she was right—Orion, rising,
is more blueprint of butterfly, or bird,
than hunter. How does it enter, through what rift
or flaw? Maybe it doesn't enter at all.
It was there in every sentence: the end.

EDITH SWAN-NECK

King Harald's face having been so disfigured in the battle, the body could be identified
with certainty only by his mistress, Edith Swan-Neck, who recognized her lover by a
certain mark, or marks, known only to herself.
        —Saxon Chronicles, 1066

                    *

> *How did I know him,   one form amid the fallen,*
> *with each gully a mass grave   or pitiful tidepool,*
> *and wails of the wounded   all tolling in babe's tongue,*
> *and faces unfeatured,   all wearing just one face?*

They dragged me out of the camp onto that part of the field where
he was last seen and said, Find him. I knelt among the bodies and
on my knees I wandered, corpse to corpse, too weary to keep rising.
So many bodies already stripped to the skin, or further. I feared to
find him that way, nameless. Did I fear death would end by toppling
him from his rank—that it would show him to be no more than
any other man? But death always does that. I found him. One of his
House Carls, dying, had draped his own body over Harald's to shield
it, mingling their limbs and gore, yet still I could make out, on a part
of Harald's body, the mark.

> *How did I know him,   that form amid the fallen—*
> *his blond-as-a-boy's hair?   (now dark with his dying)*
> *his eyes blue as islets?   (now ripped red by arrows)*
> *his fingers felt often?   (now clenched as a hawk's claw)*
> *his belly and below it?   (all naked, unknowing)*
> *by birthmark or battlescar?   (his body unblighted)*

For his body had few inborn marks, and only three small scars, until this last clash marred and engraved it with manmade ones. I knew him all the same. I had made a mark of my own, never mind just where, to this very end: so I might pick him from among the dead.

And I did. But I said nothing.

Another woman might have marked him because, begrudging him to dead battle-mates, she would have wished to take him back in the end and bury him in a place of her own. But I didn't begrudge him; and the enemy, I knew, would never let me pick his place of burial. And if he was not to lie by me in bed that night, or beside me in the earth through the coming winters, I would not stand for the enemy planting him somewhere in this pilfered land like a rune, a shrine to their win and our loss. In farewell, I fingered the mark on his body and trudged away on my knees and before long, nearby, picked another man—one of the earls, likewise slashed and bloodied and hard to know by sight, and I wept and tore at my hair and lied to them that this was Harald.

Whose true grave is easily found: acres wide, filled with bones, a slash the earth will not soon heal. I go there often, with Harald's dogs.

READING *THE SAXON CHRONICLES*
IN A FIELD HOSPITAL, KANDAHAR

Wounded, you wonder: could your own wife
have picked you from the ranks? Private
volumes defaced by night's postscript falling
or by wounds—lit in fits by the flaring
exclamation points
of mortar rounds—
                    Stripped to the equivocal voiceprint
of cough or moan, could you be known?
Weird triage: a test of past attention.
Did she read you (all those hours)
letter by letter, cell by syllable, or
were you skimmed, skipped over—never
pored through and devoured in bed, lamp fierce,
deep into the years?
                    And woman, would he know you
by the vellum texture of skin, sewn binding of bone,
spine, embossing or Braille of birthmark, scar?
(Or by hands, surely those, wrist, nipples, pubis,
angle of hip?) Were you a loved volume
or leaflet? Daybook left in a mind's drawer
or book of psalms?
                    Take me up,
spread me open to the last place, and sing.

ELEGY FOR A SURVIVOR

Olive, lady
of a dozen names, alias
Lydia Alydia Olivia, all
alive like you and still now
numbered among olives
not for the bitter
but the strong—

At gatherings you were worth a dozen guests, O., with no
malice making spectres
of your retinue—an aristocrat of the affections, like fiction's
Lady Brett
but clear-hearted, with a comprehensive soul—hyperbolic
inside our lives
those brilliant paired summers lush enough, like you, with life
that now your death
seems so odd a fit, no coffin could be heartwood or deep enough carapace
(though it gapes now
too spacious for what remains). Still, tonight, I wonder how I hope
to hold you—*you,* I mean,
the vital quorum absent at the closing—in the vespiary of a poem
with its minor hum,
its foolscap walls—and racing these lines to the deaf precipice
of the margin, I'm afraid stalling

even a breath, haemorrhaging momentum, would be to lose this vestige
I mean to hold hostage
a double deeper into the night: You and those anonymous, guerrilla
sprees of gift-leaving, star anise, blood
persimmons, cardamom pods in a bag by the door (final self
portrait in perishables) or this
neural triptych I upload: hair rowelled around your face on a midnight
river milted with stars: you
winning rounds of Twister in a timewarp rec-room: and last week,
finally, weighing not a pound
for each year of yours on earth, flirting with that handsome orderly
and begging him for Breakthrough.

O., something about your going now hatchets me open
in a one-time way, I guess
we owe it to the dead to deserve our lives, praise
something for the savour
of almonds, wine, olives, and other
tributes on the tongue —

I

Her coffin is lowered: lifeboat over a ship's rail.
We look on, a thinning crew.

2

A dream of cemetery, its upper dermis peeled back:
skeletal ranks lying in their ribs, lost
armada on the floor of the sea.

3

The rudder, torn from the boat, is free like the dead
not to steer but be borne.

ON A CHANGE OF ADDRESS CARD
SENT A FEW WEEKS BEFORE YOU DIED

I suppose, Aunt Bette, you will have sent
many like this: the NEW ADDRESS you list, almost
illegibly, is one you just passed through, en route
to a lasting address. Like most of the stressed

people who fill out these chits, Aunt
Bette, you leave the OLD ADDRESS slot
blank, presumably the recipient
already knows that one, and if not

why would they need it now? No one
needs it now. It's just this sort of official
redundancy you'd always impatiently shun—
or so I guess, not having known you well

enough, while knowing you each year of my life,
since I grew aware I had a life, you letting us
loaf at your bar like grownups, safe
from the hypothermic surf we'd just

"survived" (a sister and I in the shallows
of Trout Lake), as you boiled slabs of Baker's
Chocolate in milk, Maria Callas
shrilling from the hi-fi, to make us

hot drinks; chain-smoking, raucous
with laughter, grilling orange-
cheddar sandwiches on rye; you with grievous
bruises under the eyes, strange

badges to me then (seeming to fit the word
widow), though at some point I heard of
your "epic insomnia"—another chord
between our lives, like the love

for Pushkin you passed to me, and Robeson,
and the dreamtime deserts of The Centre,
where at nineteen I would wander
with a pack, never seeing the reason

(obvious, now) I'd chosen *there* was what I
heard at the bar—of the Martian-
red plains of Nullarbor, salt-lakes of Kiti,
legends of the Bunyip, the Southern Ocean.

Ignorance of what formed and cast oneself
across worlds is a kind of freedom, no doubt,
but to saunter inside myths of Self-
making is just life without gratitude,

or form. In those free seasons I liked to pretend
I'd no address, no author. Now I seem to yearn
to fill out a form, backdated to then—
your name (and others). Last time we went:

"I think I'm ready for something a bit more
permanent," you said, winking, even then en route
to this culminating locale, where your
husband has long been established, Bette,

and I've come to see you, dwelling now
not far from my mother, under flower-
red chestnuts that, as a child, you never knew
down under, while stars with names you never

did quite learn now bloom, perennial, above.
SPEERS, BEECHWOOD, Chestnut Lane,
Row Number 17,
Plot 5.

You could have danced more and filled fewer spreadsheets,
feared time less—not cordoned yourself in these clock-
quartz cells with the blind broker, whose costive thoughts
log overtime and follow the Dow (and lesser sites)
where even the parasites have parasites.
. Don't buy into this futures
                     "paradise,"
all the time there is is here, and skeptics, too,
sometimes recant, return to life in the current.

If your malaise isn't viral, why does it keep vectoring
south like an avian plague? I protest the repealed siestas
of Rhodes, Rome and Oaxaca—all that olive-
scented slumber and shuttered ecstasy, lost—
                            little skinflint—
don't go back to your screen, we've a flat-top guitar
and medicinal Scotch. Your soul may be a hoarder's gated hovel
but I love you, even spent. Skeptics, too, sometimes repent,
return to song in the timeless.

ICE STORM, DESERT LAKE

Seesaw sudden flight—this white-
    tail buck, through hemlocks cased
        in ice sarcophagi.

4

WHAT KEEPS YOU HERE

Somewhere in the distance
You and I had fought the monster to a draw.
—Paul Siebel

Nothing fills the famished chasm. Drape its walls with degrees,
blue ribbons, ego's little
luxury supplies —
cram it with Chairs of this or that, titles,

money — or, if not, then surely love? Of a lifetime
friend? Still no,
not quite. A husband — wife?
Or child, that love free of fine print or proviso?

For all it should, not yet. Zero fills the famished chasm.
Say as much, then go down inside
and sit there a time. It's a womb
in form, but this time in you, and so far barren. Be quiet. Reside

nowhere else for hard trimesters. If the space is dry, replenish it with
the amniotic brine of tears
long due, then learn to breathe
the green element beyond speech, as ego sputters, slowly tires

and drowns, and something else of you
readies for the immense and wave-like
labour that remains —

DREAM

Octaves woke him to dusk, not dawn —
a woman under the sealed window, singing,
woke him to sadness six years long, and lawns
of broadloom, spilled wine, the small
white pillows of sleeping pills. What
is she singing now,
where could this be?
Should have begun life years ago
instead of at some address
to come (in a desert
under a waif of moon),
                              you are the least
part of the planet, littlest
of the sallow grass.
                    Learn from the new
and uncomfortable angels.

He was tired, the gloss
had gone off the day,
but there was still the dog,
pacing, appearing at his desk
in indicting silence, with that chafing
yet stoical stare—the dog drawing him
on and out into day's dimming aftermath, earth
turning its face from the sun's latest extinction
as he and the dog plod, side by side, out of the city
into cityless time—the reliquary forest still cached
with ancestral smells, where the reviving man and
would-be-wolf (loping ahead, nose low, feverishly
truffling the cedar duff) truly run now, as if hounding more
than phobic voles, squirrels and the gone worlds hunkered
in either mind, like the first hunter and wolf to run in squadron,
before any farm or village, mill, metropolis or bylaw—all the
sensible taming and setting-to-good-use, those leashes
we're linked to, our PIN-tinkling collars and other losses
and gains. Yet for now all losses lag behind him
and the dog with her panting grin, full gallop, his pulse
pacing hard, fired up, keeping stride—deeper
into stands of pine and the great, sky-
rooted oaks, along fading, finally
untakable trails, her tail—as he
slows now, stumps in pursuit—
almost lost, a hinge of smoke
in the gloom receding
ahead into the past—

Toussaint Louverture lay in his funeral finery
while the boy locals took in the cup finals,
their bland backs crammed into the doorway
of a sports bar on Spadina, while I wheeled the hero on his gurney
(still exuding, in death, the old nimbus of yearning),
his flesh blemished by the one flukey wound
I'd bestowed.
     In those days I could never recall
how I'd killed what I'd killed, what a luxury,
the unmindful life: the lie you believed
in the telling, the crime you blandly disowned (or forgot),
your life a parkway of unmarked graves—
speed bumps barely felt through the tires—and you
yourself (fading face, and remains) isn't it true
you kept slaves?
     Really we're a rotten tribe
or just *slow*—reluctant evolutionaries—
slipping back each step like tourists on a dune
of ashes, bonemeal, bound, maybe,
for some half-hallowed future, though for now
I trolley you (transforming
as we roll through Chinatown's
gauntlet of apothecaries) up the ward corridors
these streets are, where the streetcars
judder the ground like Panzers,
where Hummers, indignant, grit their grilles,
flaring halogen eyes like demons
in a desert tapestry—

SKY BURIAL, THE SCHOLAR

In that dream, scavengers
bore his skeleton into the sky
piecemeal,

disarticulate and silenced, save
for the sighs of the ventriloquist wind
in hollowed ulna,

susurrations in the radius,
a femoral music, a marrow
of music—and he no more

than those tunnelling tunes, Self
and the elements
unsundered at last, skull's oubliette

unlocked, cracked
like the clamshell a kittiwake
lets fall over rocks——

and this is the eventual
ecstasy of skeptics——
those who swapped the rush of being

in earth's brief, arduous eden
for bunkered years in solitary,
imposing self-sentence

sentence by sentence,
who loved things only
aslant, never with the heart

full-frontal, who never once
forgot their own names when sea-
or skinscapes intervened,

never saw (eyes lasered
clear of the cataracts
of habit) rain

falling like a ransom, stars
stammering celestial news,
and the old moon, reminted.

A MONSOON SUICIDE

After gestures by Weldon Kees & Edvard Munch

In this hired room, my window
gives onto shredded sea, intruding

slats between stanzas of foam,
those lines of breakers, scrolling

slowly into noise. The window's sealed
to cut the roar, but the woman who came

with the room has brought the sea
within (her salt, her soft, nautical snores)

while out there the plying and replying
surf goes on erasing the littoral, the break-

water barely holding. Some dreams drift me
outward like a liminal form

into winds that are deafening the shore
and land: a note of departure I've been

nearing from the first, by instalment
like the tides, at a leased window, giving

onto perpetuity. *Do I miss the earth?* If she
woke, we might speak. Let in the storm.

I will. For fear this sill will rust and freeze,
lips locked after the words are done.

                              Crack
through the spaces lean out and scream——

DREAM OF FULL WAKING

In the stations
of a cortical storm, the solo
sea, plying

and replying through perilous
turnstiles in the mind, unmoors,
makes for the skyline, where

new shores are rolled of gold chain
in three strands
by the moonlight

One more time the waters of her eyes,
                              of pumice-black isles
in the iris I am sailing south through
                              in a *meltémi* of light
on a morning masked in dual moods:
                              sails luffing and the choral
keening of the shrouds, in descant,
                              the engine seized, bathymeter
mystified, losing count of the abyss,
                              and the calendar
from another June and journey—

One more time the waters of her eyes,
                              since love can always bear
another testing, can even crack
                              into strange new strengths
that barely resemble love, but might be
                              a sterner sort of learning—

because she could sightread and sing
                              the starling arpeggios
dense as Tchaikovsky, where birds
                              in intelligent scads
perched on parallel wires
                              over the harbour,

one more time the waters of her eyes
                         stir to this passage, and after it
close—now awakened to love,
                  now asleep to its swells—
so love through its cycles will sail
                   thru boulder-rooted, bare Cyclades—
so for another June and journey
                we marry, part, and remarry.

BASEBALL GAME, HAVANA

For G. B., on his seventieth

Bottom of the seventh and nothing at stake—
Industriales clinched, Cienfuegos
out of the race. A season's last innings. At most
a thousand fans in this stadium that holds

forty times that, easy, some nights. A day-game
in the violent, vertical light, squelching heat. The crowd,
though hometown, hushed. Batters, drooping drunk
with apathy, take loose, languid swings, strike out,

lounge off the field. Fielders stand lank, hips canted
like barrio girls leaning on a wall. The losers, in black,
as if grieving the season or a teammate's death,
slump from dugout onto field, slump back after yielding

two more runs. Home 12, Cienfuegos 2. So there'll be no
bittersweet last rally, no faint fleck of pride
clawed back from failure. The City of a Hundred Fires
won't go down in defiant flame, but whispering, softly,

uncle. Bottom of the ninth. In Cavafy's famous lines
on Thermopylae, the Spartans, fighting on with the result
foregone, pinch-hit for whoever lives tall, straight-hearted,
a right life, though seeing ("and many do foresee")

how things are going to end. Those Spartans brushing out
their long hair in the dawn as they await the last Persian
surge. Such *tharos*, such splendid vanity! But so many
live this fainter way—some widowers, a certain friend

gutted by love, another by grievance, in mid-game
toe-tagged in a morgue of remorse, routine, shuffling on
through the latter stretch because one does
and maybe a few distracted viewers

in the end-blues, munching peanuts out of paper cones,
bear witness. We've been on that field too—
in the gloom between books, in illness—and so the game
goes, not in creaturely delight, devotion, a good childhood's

prolonged inebriation, but less
                              So let something
remain of the next play's possible delight—
as it has, I think, for you. Deep in the seventh, still,
to burn for a next turn at the plate.

BALLAD OF THE SLOW ROAD

The slow road is the route for you
though you'd hoped for smoother, quicker—
to skip the Chilkoot, cruise the freeway—
false hope is a fast talker.

Long's the lone road worth the going
though the work might seem for ashes
as years compound and all that accrues
are exponential wishes—

but to look your hunger in the eye
and to stare it straight to zero
and then to learn to love the wait
till the love is in your marrow

and the wait is no delay, but more
a seasoning of the will—
at no one's pace but yours, your trail
and your own shoes to fill.

WORLD ENOUGH

A ruckus
of ravens
dubundo
over the nuisance grounds

where every trace
of us two (save
what the grave
grabs) ends up—

everything is
rental, everything
is lent, ex-
piring, the thrilling

Jag, liver-
spotted, lichened
with rust,
the dream house

passing through these
hands to ex-
ecutors, like our lease-
to-lose

allotment of carbon
moving on
as it must
(even dust

falls to dust).
We own so little
of ourselves, how
did we think to own

anything of the world?
A momentary estate—
and yet, for all that,
all things here,

even the dumpsite
and the creosote
ravens, seem this sunrise
startled into being, coined

and kenned
to a newness—in chorus
with chaos—
this ruckus of birds

centrifugal
as red-shifted stars
in a cosmos
unfinished unfolding.

FALL CANVAS

She must be colour-
blind, to keep singing this way,
final cicada.

5

FOURTEEN APPROXIMATIONS

Every poem is a failed translation
—Robert Kroetsch

SILENTIUM

Fyodor Tyutchev: 1830

Don't speak. Stay hidden and withhold
all word of your thoughts, your dreams. Sealed
in the soul's cosmos, let them sail
like stars, through private skies, then fall
from sight before the dawn, unmarred.
Savour their arc. Don't say a word.

How can your heart pin down the phrase
by which it might be grasped? We lose,
in translation, the worlds we know.
Say a thing and it turns untrue
and leaves the deep spring's face sound-scarred.
Drink from the source. Don't say a word.

Learn to live in the self's retreat —
a cosmos forms there, where the light
can't force its way and where no sound
drowns out the spell of singing mind
and leaves it dazzled, deaf, unheard.
Take in the song. Don't say a word.

THINGS

Jorge Luis Borges

This cane, loose change, my ring of keys,
this trusty lock, belated notes which the short
time left to me will leave no time to peruse,
the deck of cards and the checkerboard,
a book, and in its pages a shrivelled flower,
memento of an afternoon that was surely
unforgettable (forgotten now, however),
this west-facing mirror, violet with the fiery
show of an illusory dawn. How many things—
doorsills, doornails, mapbooks, wineglasses, tongs—
slave their lives away in our service, taciturn,
unseeing, so inscrutably reserved . . .
they will endure beyond our own going
and they will never realize we are gone.

REMORSE

Jorge Luis Borges

I stand guilty of the worst sin any man
can commit. I've failed to be happy.
Let the glaciers of oblivion
bear me off and bury me— no pity.
My parents gave me breath so I could leap
bare into life's daring, gorgeous game, and savour
the earth: its rivers, winds, and anthered fire.
I've defrauded them. I wasn't happy. The hopes
of their joining lie squandered, my mind given
to such sterile symmetries as *these* careful
lines—High Art, weaving trifles from trifles.
They bequeathed me courage. I was craven.
Yet I'm not alone, for it's always close by me,
this shadow of having been a man of sighs.

SONG FOR SENNA'S EYES

J. E. Villalta

When I came
without Senna, her name
surprised me, surging from
my throat and tongue—

how I loved the shadows under Senna's eyes.

And her thighs
clamped round my ears
so that her flesh, for an hour,
shut out the world, I

loved the shadows under Senna's eyes.

And our mutely sung
duet of tongue
on tongue, not in staved
harmony but unison—how I loved

the shadows under Senna's eyes!

Now with Senna gone, my mind feigns
calm, but body runs
in sleep to find her,
as if not yet resigned, nor ever—
how I loved the shadows under
Senna's eyes!

THE PEACOCK

Guillaume Apollinaire

Splaying his tail, this exceptional fowl
    whose jewelled plumage shames the August grass
      enhances his splendour—seems almost royal—
but also exposes his common ass.

NOON ON EARTH!

starting from Horace, i, 11

Why trouble wondering how long
breath will last, how long your eyes
will still bask in the heavenshed
lucence of noon on earth. Horoscopes,
palmistry, the seance gild pockets
but confide nothing sure. We have to take it—
the future's shrugged *whatever*, that weather
of uncertainty—unknowing whether gods
will grant us the grey of further
winters that'll churn the sea until the sea
gnaws, noses into the littoral
of our lives, eroding whatever is
so far unclaimed.
                  Enough.
Better open the red, pitch the cork, toast
our moment—tomorrow's an idle
nevering, ghost of a god
unworth such wasted faith.

"A STRANGE FASHION OF FORSAKING . . ."

Horace i, 25: via Thomas Wyatt

The wilder girls hardly bother anymore
to rattle your shuttered window with fists, or
pitch stones, shatter your dreamfree sleep, while your door,
    once oiled and swinging,

nimbly hinged, hangs dead with rust. Less and less
often you wake to ex-lovers crying, "Thomas,
you bastard, how can you sleep?—I'm dying for us
    to do it again."

Seems to me your turn's long overdue— solo
nightshift when, like some codger in a cul-
de-sac, you'll moan for all the women (scornful
    now) who one time sought you.

The cold will be what finds you then—northeasters
whining down in the gloom of the moon, and lust
in riddled guts twisting you like a stud in must
    who has to stand watching

his old mares mounted. You'll know then, the desire
of girls is for greener goods—such dry sticks
and wiltwood, blown only by the cold, they just figure
    who has the time for.

TANKAS

Onakatomi no Yoshinobu: c. 950

1

The lone doe that lives
among the mountains of pine
where no leaves fall
can know the autumn has come
by her own cry alone.

2

The guardfires that burn
at the imperial gate—
embering all day
and then, at nightfall, flaring—
such is the love that glows in me.

LOVE SONNET XVII

Pablo Neruda

I love you not as if you were topaz, a saline
rose, quiverful of carnations strewing flame— ,
I love you in secrecy, as one loves certain
unclear things, between shadow and the soul. No bloom

on the plant I love as I love you, which retains,
interred in itself, the light of its lost blossoms,
while in my flesh the dense, ascending fragrance
earth generates now darkly resides, by reason

of your love. I love you without knowing how, when,
where from, I love you straight on, no complication
or pride, love you like this because I've never known

another way to love: *you* and *I* have no more meaning,
so close that your hand on my body is my own,
so close now your eyelids close with my sleeping.

LAMENT FOR A MOTHER, 1961

Stamatis Smyrlis

In birth, un-
conscious, I
forced these scars.

Unconscious
in dying, you
return the pain.

Returned, I sob
like a newborn,
yours.

FRAGMENTS OF A VOYAGE

I

Gale-borne toward new shorelines forever
in the harbourless night, without pause, washed away—
on this ocean of ages, why may we never
drop anchor for a single day?

2

Now the crewmen sit to their oars in order and slip
the cable from the bollard hole and heave backwards
so their oarblades chop at the swell and churn up water
while over the captain sweet sleep irresistibly
falls so fathomless and sound it might almost be the sleep
of death itself. And the ship like a team of stallions
coursing to the crack of the lash with hoofs bounding
high and manes blown back foamlike off the summits of waves
lunges along stern up and plunging as the riven
rollers close up crashing together in her wake
and she surges on so unrelenting not even a bird
quick as the falcon could have stayed abreast. . . .
So she leaps on splitting the black combers bearing
a man who has suffered years of sorrow and turmoil
until his heart grew weary of scything a path home
through his enemies, or the furious ocean. . . .

3

A song I can shape you—   my story of sailing
and travel sing truly—   how often outlasting
struggle and hardship,   heart-straining days
I bitterly abided   and bore, in my sorrow,
full cargos of cares.   I've known my hull cumbered
while surf in its seizures   clawed at the ship's prow
so I on the nightwatch   was often tormented.
As we pitched athwart cliffs   I, fettered by hoarfrost
and clamped to the deckboards,   my feet in ice shackles,
felt only my heart hot   with fear seething round it
while hunger gnawed outward   consuming both body
and seawearied soul.

      Landsmen know little
of their luck not to sail here,   to rest on the shoreline,
while I, raked by sorrows   on the icewater sea,
must outweather winters   in regions of exile,
by kin uncompanioned,   where icicles dangle
and hail drives like iron,   with nothing to hear except
seas in their heaving   and the glacier wave.
At times the swan's wail
I hold to my heart now;   in lieu of men's laughter
the clangour of gannets   and curlew for laughter;
the mewing of seagulls   for the drinking of mead.

4

At sea, storms hallowed my night-watches with joy;
lighter than a cork I danced over waves known
as the unceasing rollers of drowned men, ten
nights, never missing the vapid eyes of the quay-

lanterns in port. Sweet as the tart flesh of green
apples to a child, the salt water seeped through my
pinewood hull, rinsed splotches of vomit and cyan wine
clean off me, tore my anchor and rudder away.

And ever since that time I've bathed in the poem
of the sea, steeped and milky with stars, guzzling
the green azures, where at times the ecstatic flotsam
of a drowned man, pale and pensive, will be sinking. . . .

5

But those journeys had no harbours. As time passed
my crewmen seemed to merge with the oars—pulsing
dip and heft of oarlocked oars—their iced
or sun-seared features seeming to mirror
the painted prow's stern features, while the waking
sea, athwart and astern, riled up by rudder
and sea-trowelling blade, gave back their likeness
too. Man by man my Argonauts slipped to slumber,
left the benches empty. Each now rests ashore,
his final berth there marked by his oar.

And no one remembers their names. Justice

I: Alphonse de Lamartine, from "The Lake"; 2: Homer, from *The Odyssey*,
Book XIII; 3: from *The Seafarer* (anonymous Anglo-Saxon); 4: Arthur
Rimbaud, from *Le Bateau Ivre*; 5: George Seferis, from "Argonauts."

LIFE!

after Miltos Sahtoúris

Night in the all-night
drug mart
where a kneeling
horse
devours
the vinyl tile
and a woman
with curious vernal burns
is being treated
urgently
while the
ghost despairingly
weeps
by the magazines

ANGUISH

Stéphane Mallarmé

I'm not here to master your body, Creature
teeming with a people's sins, or to sow
sad monsoons tonight in your filthy hair
out of the chronic ennui my kiss let flow —
of your bed, I ask stone sleep, and dreamless
soaring in furtive curtains of remorse,
a sleep you can taste after your darkest lies —
you who know oblivion better than the dead.

Eating away my inborn virtue, Vice
marks me, like yourself, with its barrenness —
but your breast of stone still retains the grace
of a heart unbitten by the least offence,
while I flee, stalked by a shroud of my own,
frightened of dying when I sleep alone.

ELEGY

Wang Wei: c. 756

We returned with your body
    to bury you
        high on Mount Shih-lou

and after, through stands of ever-
    green and oak, we rode back
        home to our lives.

Your bones stay behind
    to whiten under clouds
        until the end of time

and there is only the river that flows on
    down to the world of men.

"Another of the Just: Warrant Officer Hugh Thompson, My Lai, 1968": Thompson's two crewmen were Glenn Andreotta, who was killed in action three weeks after the My Lai incident, and Lawrence Colburn, who survived the war, who was at Thompson's side when he died of cancer in 2006, and who attended a 40th anniversary commemoration of the massacre, at the site, on March 16, 2008.

The proximate source of the phrase "my sad captain" is Thom Gunn's poem "My Sad Captains"; the ultimate source is Walt Whitman's phrase (and title) "O Captain! My Captain!" from his elegy for Abraham Lincoln, collected in the 1900 edition of *Leaves of Grass*.

"Ribs" is for Paul Quarrington.

"The Neither Life": The italicized epigraph, from chapter one of Marina Tsvetaeva's long poem *The Ratcatcher*, is taken from Elaine Feinstein's superb translation in *Marina Tsvetaeva: Selected Poems* (Penguin Classics, 1994).

"Some Other Just Ones": The poem's italicized first and last lines are translated from Jorge Luis Borges's poem "The Just."

"Thar He": The title of the poem quotes Moses Wright, the prosecution's chief witness against Roy Bryant and his brother-in-law, J. W. Milam, at the two men's 1956 trial for the murder of 14-year-old Emmett Till. Till, from Chicago, was visiting a cousin in Money, Mississippi, when he was abducted, tortured and murdered by Bryant and Milam, allegedly for flirting with Bryant's wife. In the courtroom, Moses Wright identified Bryant by pointing at him—a moment captured in a remarkable photograph—and saying, "Thar he" (sometimes transliterated "Dar he"). The all-white jury acquitted the accused. Under the double jeopardy provision of U.S. law, the two men could never be tried again for the same crime, so they sold a detailed, unapologetic account of their actions to *Look* magazine for $4,000.

The victim's mother, Mamie Till-Mobley, is credited with helping to ignite and energize the civil rights movement by insisting on a public viewing of her son's grotesquely disfigured corpse during the funeral in Chicago, where as many as fifty thousand people may have passed the coffin.

"Not the Kind to Die": On June 10, 2009, James Von Brunn, an 88-year-old white supremacist and Holocaust denier, entered the Holocaust Memorial Museum in Washington, D.C., and shot dead the African-American guard who had just held the door for him. The other guards then opened fire on Von Brunn, gravely wounding him; he was hospitalized and for some weeks remained in critical condition. In September 2009, somewhat recovered, he made his first court appearance.

"The Mascot": Commissioned for *Telling Stories, Secret Lives*, a collaborative exhibition at the Agnes Etherington Art Gallery, Kingston, Ontario. The poem responds to an installation by Mfanwy MacLeod.

"Election Night Dream, November 2008": Toussaint Louverture was the charismatic and visionary leader of the Haitian Revolution (1791–1804).

"Deathbed Lament, 1961": Stamatis Smyrlis is the *nom de plume* of the Greek poet Stratis Apanopolis (1939–).

"Song for Senna's Eyes": J.E. Villalta, thought by some to have been a sort of escaped and renegade heteronym of Fernando Pessoa, was actually a Spanish poet who published only one book, *Canciónes y otras canciónes*, and who, while continuing to write in Spanish, lived in Rio Tinto, Portugal for most of his life (1907–1988).

Versions of some of the poems in this book were first published in the magazines and anthologies listed below. The author is very grateful to the editors.

Arc
The Best Canadian Poetry 2009 (ed. A. F. Moritz)
Brick
The Exile Book of Poems in Translation (ed. Priscila Uppal)
Geist
Lichen
London Magazine
London Review of Books
The Malahat Review
The New Quarterly
Poetry London
PRISM *International*
Richard Outram: Essays on His Work (ed. Ingrid Ruthig)
Scapes (ed. Diane Dawber)
The Sea, A Literary Companion (ed. Wayne Grady)
Telling Stories, Secret Lives (ed. Jan Allen)
The Walrus
71 (+) for George Bowering (ed. Jean Baird)

"Some Other Just Ones" was broadcast on the BBC radio program *Something Understood* and on the BBC World Service, April 2009.

I also want to thank by name the people who commented on one or a number of the poems as they evolved: above all, my editor and friend Ken Babstock, as well as Mary Huggard, Michael Holmes, Ingrid Ruthig, Alvin Lee, Kim Jernigan, Helga Grodzinski,

Carolyn Smart, Jenny Haysom, Jason Guriel, Jay Ruzesky, Jennifer Duncan, Don Coles, Robyn Sarah, Amanda Jernigan, Mary Cameron, Michael Hurley, Michael Redhill, A. F. Moritz, Elisabeth Harvor, Jay Rogoff, and Alexander Scala.

Over the last couple of years, I've been lucky to serve as a writer-in-residence at the University of Ottawa and at McArthur College, Queen's University. My thanks to the residency organizers and to the institutions themselves. Finally, a thank you to the Ontario Arts Council for its support of these poems.

This book is for John and Christina Heighton.

S. H., Kingston, November 2009

AUTHOR PHOTOGRAPH: © MARY HUGGARD

STEVEN HEIGHTON is the author of the novels *Afterlands*, a *New York Times Book Review* Editors' Choice and a best of year selection in ten publications in Canada, the US, and the UK; *The Shadow Boxer*, a Canadian bestseller and a *Publishers Weekly* book of the year; and *Every Lost Country*, which will be published in spring 2010. He has also published four poetry collections, including *Stalin's Carnival*, which won the Gerald Lampert Memorial Award; *The Ecstasy of Skeptics*, a Governor General's Literary Award finalist; and *The Address Book*, poems from which received the Petra Kenney Prize and gold in the National Magazine Awards. His poems and short stories have appeared in such magazines and anthologies as *Poetry, London Review of Books, Tin House, The Walrus, Europe, Agni, Poetry London, Brick, Canadian Short Fiction,* and *Best English Stories*. He lives in Kingston, Ontario.